THE   WAY   OF   HOLINESS

THE WAY OF HOLINESS

BY

COMMISSIONER S. L. BRENGLE, D.D., O.F.

1980 Edition
Published by
THE SALVATION ARMY
SUPPLIES AND PURCHASING DEPARTMENT
Atlanta, Georgia

First Published in 1902

ISBN: 0-86544-008-5

Printed in the United States of America

PREFACE TO THE FIRST EDITION

THIS BOOK has been written at my request. I have read it with thankfulness to God. I feel that in its preparation He has evidently helped and influenced the author who is an officer of The Salvation Army at present labouring in the United States of America and the writer of two other useful publications on the same subject: namely, ' Helps to Holiness ' and ' Heart-Talks on Holiness,' both of them in our ' Red-Hot Library.'

What subject can be either of greater importance or interest to our young people for whom ' The Warriors' Library ' is especially intended than holiness? The notion that the deep things of God are only open to the experienced and the wise has, surely, no longer any place among us. It is in the mouths of babes He has perfected praise; it is those who seek that find, whatever their age or history or worldly wisdom may be; and a full salvation, so greatly needed by those who have to find their way amid the pitfalls and allurements of youth, is provided for them all in the unsearchable riches of the grace of God. It is the common heritage of every soldier of Christ.

A holy life is a life given to God and accepted by Him. He is the holy man who lives no more to himself; who lives no longer for his own will or in the way or spirit of the world, but who lives to God and in His will; who loves and obeys Him, considers and serves Him in everything, and who makes all the common, as well as the sacred things of his life honour his Lord by doing them in such a manner as pleases Him. To help every reader of this book to understand and experience this is the purpose for which it has been written.

But that purpose will not be attained without sincerity in the reader. Religion is in very large measure a matter of motive and intention. If you are really as forward in the life of God as you can be, if you have set your heart upon an entire conformity to His will and are seeking it day and night, then, notwithstanding many defects and imperfections, your Master will bless and reward you; but if your weakness and unbelief, your want of humility and courage and love are the fruits of your own neglect, and the want of a sincere determination to be a holy servant of God, then you have no more excuse for your falls and failures than have those who commit open and shameful sins.

I call you then, while you read here the counsels of the Spirit of Jesus speaking through His servant, to make up your mind to live a holy life, to resolve that by the power of the Holy Ghost you will work out your own salvation and walk the world in white.

BRAMWELL BOOTH.

LONDON.

April, 1902.

CONTENTS

CHAPTER I

WHAT IS HOLINESS?

A NUMBER of years ago, before many of the young people for whom this book is written were born, a girl asked me, ' What is this sanctification, or holiness, that people are talking so much about? '

She had heard the experience testified to and talked and preached about for nearly a year, until I thought that, of course, she understood it. Her question surprised and almost discouraged me, but I rallied and asked, ' Have you a bad temper? '

' Oh, yes,' she said, ' I have a temper like a volcano.'

' Sanctification,' I replied, ' is to have that bad temper taken out.' That definition set her thinking and did her good; but it was hardly accurate. If I had said, ' Sanctification is to have our sinful tempers cleansed, and the heart filled with love to God and man,' that would have done, for that is sanctification, that is holiness. It is, in our measure, to be made like God. It is to be made ' partakers of the divine nature ' (2 Pet. i. 4).

A spark from the fire is like the fire. The tiniest twig on the giant oak, or the smallest branch of the vine, has the nature of the oak or the vine, and is in that respect like the oak or the vine. A drop of water on the end of your finger from the ocean is like the ocean: not in its size, of course, for the big ships cannot float upon it nor the big fishes swim in it; but it is like the ocean in its essence, in its character, in its nature. Just so, a holy person is like God. Not that he is infinite as God is; he does not know everything; he has not all power and wisdom as God has; but he is like God in his nature.

He is good and pure and loving and just, in the same way that God is.

Holiness, then, is conformity to the nature of God. It is likeness to God as He is revealed in Jesus.

But some one will cry out: ' Impossible! We are poor sinful creatures. We cannot be like Jesus. He was divine. Show me a man like Jesus Christ.'

Well, now, let us be patient, keep quiet, go to the Bible and see what that says about the matter before we further define holiness. What did Jesus Himself say? Listen!

1. In speaking of the separation of His disciples from the world, Jesus says, ' They are not of the world, even as I am not of the world.' And again, 'As Thou hast sent Me into the world, even so have I also sent them into the world ' (John xvii. 16, 18). We are, then, to be like Jesus in separation from the world. Jesus was in the world but He was not of the world. He took no pleasure in its wicked ways. He was not spoiled at all by its proud, sinful, selfish spirit. While He worked and associated with bad people to do them good, yet He was always separate from them in spirit.

One of our dear, good rescue officers went to a brothel to see a sick girl. While she was there the health authorities declared the girl's sickness to be smallpox and sealed up the place. The officer was shut in for weeks among those poor lost women. She was in an evil place but she was not of it. Her pure spirit was utterly opposed to the spirit of sin that ruled there. So Jesus was in the world but not of it; and in the same way, holy people are so changed that while they are in the world they are not of it. They belong to Heaven and are but strangers and pilgrims, doing all the good they can while passing through this world to their Father's house, their Heavenly Home. They are separate from the world.

2. The Apostle John, in speaking of those who expect to see Jesus and to be like Him in Heaven says, 'And every man that hath this hope in Him purifieth himself,

even as He is pure' (1 John iii. 3). That is a lofty standard of purity for there was no impurity in Jesus. He allowed no unclean habits. He indulged in no impure thoughts or desires. He used no unkind words. He kept Himself pure in all things. So we are to be pure in heart and in life as He was.

3. Again, Jesus said, in speaking of God's kindness and love for unjust and evil people, ' Be ye therefore perfect, even as your Father which is in Heaven is perfect' (Matt. v. 48).

Again, He says, 'A new commandment I give unto you, that ye love one another.' How? According to what standard? 'As I have loved you, that ye also love one another' (John xiii. 34). We are, then, to be like Jesus in love to God and to all men, even to our enemies, but especially to our brothers and sisters in the Lord.

4. In speaking of Himself, Jesus says, ' Believe Me that I am in the Father, and the Father in Me' (John xiv. 11). And then He says of His disciples, 'At that day' (the day of Pentecost when the Comforter comes) ' ye shall know that I am in My Father, and ye in Me, and I in you' (John xiv. 20). We are, then, to be like Jesus by having God dwelling in us.

So we see that the Bible teaches that we can be like Jesus. We are to be like Him in our separation from the world, in purity, in love, and in the fullness of the Spirit. This is holiness.

This work was begun in you when you were converted. You gave up your sins. You were in some measure separated from the world, the love of God was in some degree shed abroad in your heart, and you felt that God was with you. But unless you have been sanctified wholly, you also feel that there are yet roots of bitterness within: quickness of temper, stirrings of pride, too great a sensitiveness to praise or blame, shame of the Cross, love of ease, worldly-mindedness, and the like. These must be taken away before your heart can be made clean, love to God and man made perfect, and the Holy Spirit have all His way in you.

When this is done, you will have the experience which the Bible calls holiness, and which The Salvation Army rightly teaches is the birthright of all God's dear children.

Holiness, then, for you and for me, is not maturity, but purity: a clean heart in which the Holy Spirit dwells, filling it with pure, tender, and constant love to God and man.

There is a plant in South America called the ' pitcher plant,' on the stalk of which, below each leaf, is a little cup-like formation which is always full of water. When it is very small it is full; as it grows larger it is still full; and when it reaches maturity it is full. That illustrates holiness. All that God asks is that the heart should be cleansed from sin and full of love, whether it be the tender heart of the little child with feeble powers of loving, or of the full-grown man, or of the flaming archangel before the Throne. This is holiness, and this only. It is nothing less than this and it can be nothing more.

> Jesus, Thine all-victorious love
> Shed in my heart abroad;
> Then shall my feet no longer rove,
> Rooted and fixed in God.

CHAPTER II

WHY SHOULD WE BE HOLY?

WE should be holy because God wants us to be holy. He commands it. He says, 'As He which hath called you is holy, so be ye holy in all manner of conversation; because it is written, Be ye holy; for I am holy' (1 Pet. i. 15, 16). God is in earnest about this. It is God's will and it cannot be evaded. Just as a man wants his watch to keep perfect time, his work to be accurate, wants his friends to be steadfast, his children to be obedient, his wife to be faithful, so God wants us to be holy.

To many, however, the command seems harsh. They have been accustomed to commands accompanied by curses or kicks or blows. But we must not forget that ' God is love,' and His commands are not harsh but kind. They come from the fullness of an infinitely loving and all-wise heart. They are meant for our good. If a railway train could think or talk, it might argue that running on two rails over the same road year after year was very common-place. But if it insisted on larger liberty and jumped the track, it would certainly ruin itself. So the man who wants freedom, and refuses to obey God's commands to be holy, destroys himself. The train was made to run on the track, and we were made to live according to God's commandment to be holy. Only in that way can we gain everlasting good.

Oh, how tender are His words! Listen. 'And now . . . what doth the Lord thy God require of thee, but to fear the Lord thy God, to walk in all His ways, and to love Him, and to serve the Lord thy God with all

thy heart and with all thy soul, to keep the commandments of the Lord, and His statutes . . . for thy good?'
(Deut. x. 12, 13).

For thy good! For thy good! Do you not see it, my
brother, my sister? It is 'for thy good.' There is
nothing harsh, nothing selfish in our dear Lord's command. It is 'thy good' He is seeking. Bless His
name! 'God is love.'

We should be holy because Jesus died to make us
holy. He gave Himself to stripes and spitting and
cruel mockings, the crown of thorns and death on the
Cross for this purpose. He wants a holy people. For
this He prayed. 'Sanctify them through Thy truth:
Thy word is truth' (John xvii. 17). For this He died.
'Who gave Himself for us, that He might redeem us
from all iniquity, and purify unto Himself a peculiar
people, zealous of good works' (Titus ii. 14). He
'loved the church, and gave Himself for it; that He
might sanctify and cleanse it . . . that He might
present it to Himself a glorious church, not having spot,
or wrinkle, or any such thing; but that it should be holy
and without blemish' (Eph. v. 25–27). Let us not dis-
appoint Him. Let not His precious Blood be spent in
vain.

We should be holy in order that we may be made useful. Who have been the mightiest men of God of all the
ages? They have been holy men; men with clean
hearts on fire with love to God and man; unselfish men;
humble men who forgot themselves in their love and
toil for others; faithful men whose lives were 'hid with
Christ in God.' Moses, the meekest of men; Paul, who
would gladly pour out his life a sacrifice for the people;
Luther, Fox, St. Francis, Wesley, General and Mrs.
Booth and ten thousand times ten thousand other men
and women who were 'great in the sight of the Lord.'
These are the ones whom God has used.

So long as there are any roots of sin in the heart the
Holy Spirit cannot have all His way in us, and our
usefulness is hindered. But when our hearts are clean

the Holy Spirit dwells within, and then we have power for service. Then we can work for God, and do good in spite of all our ignorance and weakness. Hallelujah!

A plain, humble young Irishman heard about the blessing of a clean heart, and went alone and fell on his knees before the Lord, crying to Him for it. A man happened to overhear him and wrote about it, saying, ' I shall never forget his petition. " O God, I plead with Thee for this blessing!" Then, as if God was showing him what was in the way, he said, " My Father, I will give up every known sin, only I plead with Thee for power." And then, as if his individual sins were passing before him, he said again and again, " I will give them up; I will give them up."

' Then without any emotion he rose from his knees, turned his face Heavenward, and simply said, "And now, I claim the blessing." For the first time he now became aware of my presence and, with a shining face, reached out his hand to clasp mine. You could feel the presence of the Spirit as he said, " I have received Him; I have received Him!"

'And I believe he had, for in the next few months he led more than sixty men into the Kingdom of God. His whole life was transformed.'

To be holy and useful is possible for each one of us, and it is far better than to be great and famous. To save a soul is better than to command an army, to win a battle, to rule an empire or to sit upon a throne.

Again, we should be holy that we may be safe. Sin in the heart is more dangerous than gunpowder in the cellar. Before the disciples got the blessing of a clean heart and the baptism of the Holy Spirit they forsook their Master and fled.

Remember that holiness is nothing more nor less than perfect love for God and man in a clean heart. If we love God with all our heart we will gladly keep all His commandments and do all His will as He makes it known to us. And if we love our fellow-men as we love ourselves, we will not do, knowingly, any wrong to them.

B

So we see that this holy love is the surest possible safe-guard against all kinds of sin either against God or man, and we cannot count ourselves safe unless we have it. Without it, Peter and David fell; but with it, Joseph and Daniel resisted the temptations of kings' courts, and the three Hebrew children and the fire-baptized Stephen and Paul gladly faced death rather than deny their Lord.

Finally, we should be holy because we are most solemnly assured that without holiness ' no man shall see the Lord ' (Heb. xii. 14). God has made all things ready so that we may have the blessing if we will, thus leaving those who refuse or trifle and fail without excuse.

I bless Him that years ago He awakened me to the infinite importance of this matter, sent holy people to testify to and explain the experience, enabled me to consecrate my whole being to Him and seek Him with all my heart, and He gave me the blessing.

Will you have it, my comrade? If so, receive Jesus as your Sanctifier just now.

> My idols I cast at Thy feet,
>   My all I return Thee, who gave!
> This moment the work is complete,
>   For Thou art almighty to save!
>
> O Saviour, I dare to believe,
>   Thy Blood for my cleansing I see;
> And, asking in faith, I receive
>   Salvation, full, present, and free.

CHAPTER III

HOW TO GET HOLINESS

GOD never raises a crop of potatoes or a field of wheat or a bushel of oats without man's help. He takes men into partnership with Him in such matters. He furnishes the sunshine and the air, the rain and the dew, the day and the night, the fruitful seasons, the busy, burrowing little earth-worms and insects which keep the lungs of the earth open so that it can breathe. He gives life to the seed so that it may grow. Man must prepare the ground, plant the seed, keep down the weeds and gather in the harvest. Men sometimes think that they are doing it all, but they are quite mistaken in this. Our loving Heavenly Father has been preparing the earth for thousands of years for every potato that grows, and He ceaselessly works, by day and by night, to help man raise his crops.

And so it is in matters that concern our souls. God and man must work together both to save and to sanctify. God never saves a sinner without that sinner's help, and usually the help of some other folk as well, who preach or pray, write or sing or suffer that he may be saved. Ages before we were born God provided the means of salvation for all. Angels and prophets spoke God's truth. Jesus came and showed us God's love and died for our sins; the Holy Spirit was given, the blessed Bible was written and all things were made ready.

But now, the sinner must hear the truth for himself, must repent, must confess his sins and give them up, must ask God for pardon, and believe, before he can be saved. And for a sinner to expect salvation without doing this would be as big a piece of folly as for a farmer

9

to expect a crop of potatoes without having planted them.

And so, to get the priceless gift of the Holy Spirit—a clean heart—we must work together with God. On God's side all things are ready, and He waits and longs to give us the blessing, but before He can do so we must, with His help, get ourselves ready; we must do our part, which is very simple and easily within our power to do.

1. We must see our need of the blessing, and fully to see this need we must be justified. The sinner's eyes are not open to see the need of a clean heart. He is blind to these things. He may have dreadful hatred in his heart, but so long as he restrains himself and does the person he hates no harm, he thinks he is a very good sort of fellow. He cannot see that in the eyes of God he is a murderer, for does not God say, ' Whosoever hateth his brother is a murderer ' ? (1 John iii. 15). He may have lust in his heart, but so long as he does not commit adultery he flatters himself that he is quite respectable in God's sight, in spite of the fact that Jesus says that the *look* of lust is adultery.

The first thing then, is to be well saved, and so fully in the light of God's smile that we can see our need of cleansing.

2. We must not try to hide the need, but frankly confess it. Let me ask you: do you know that you are saved? You say, ' Oh, yes, I know that I have given my heart to God, and I feel that my sins have been forgiven and my life has been changed. I feel that I am saved just now.'

Good, but do you know that your heart is clean? Are all the roots of bitterness gone? Do you bear patiently the faults of others? Do you bear meekly, and with a forgiving spirit, the unkindness of others? Do you love God with all your heart and soul and mind, and your neighbour as yourself? Do you feel that all malice, pride, jealousy, envy, and evil and filthy desire, unholy ambition and unbelief, and all foolish things have been taken out of your heart; that the Holy Spirit has His own way in you all the while? Remember that holiness has to do with the heart and that, as Solomon says: Out of the heart are the issues of life. It is at the heart that Jesus looks, and He says, 'Blessed are the pure in heart' (Matt. v. 8).

Now, if your heart is not clean, do not be afraid or ashamed to say so, but frankly tell your Heavenly Father the whole truth about the matter.

3. The next thing is to believe that the blessing is for you. Of course, if you do not believe that you can be cleansed from envy and jealousy, quick temper and all sin, and be kept pure and good all the time, you will not seek for it.

Satan, surely, will do all he can to discourage you and make you doubt the possibility of holiness for yourself. He will tell you that it is for other people, but not for you. But he might as well tell you that the sun shines for other people, but not for you! Our Heavenly Father 'maketh His sun to rise on the evil and on the good, and sendeth rain on the just and on the unjust' (Matt. v. 45). He is no respecter of persons. Bless His holy name! And He offers His full salvation to all who will take it.

Satan will tell you that your disposition is so peculiar, or your circumstances at home, or at school, or in the shop, or mine, or mill, are so disagreeable that you cannot hope to be holy.

Your disposition may be peculiar, but God will take all the sin out of it, so that where it is now peculiarly impatient and jealous, envious and lustful and bad, it will be peculiarly good and patient, loving and generous and humble and chaste. A highly strung, quick-tempered girl got sanctified, and it made her gentle like Jesus. A proud, ambitious young fellow whom I know, got a clean heart, and he was made humble and self-sacrificing until his friends hardly knew him.

As for your circumstances, holiness will make you their master instead of their servant. The other day I wanted a hole in the hard rubber cap of the fountain-pen with which I am writing these words, so I heated a pin, and burned the hole right through. If the pin had been cold I should probably have broken either the pin or the cap, and should certainly have failed to make that hole. Holiness will make you hot enough to burn your way through your circumstances. ' Our God is a consuming fire,' and holiness is *God in you.*

Satan may tell you that you have failed so often that now God will not give you the blessing. That is the devil's lie. Don't believe it. Your mother might treat you in that way, but God won't, for ' God is love.' He knows all about your failures, and pities you, and loves you still, and wants to give you the blessing far more than you want to receive it. Peter failed again and again during the three years he was with Jesus, and finally there was an awful failure during that sad hour when he cursed and swore that he did not know Him. But in spite of it all, Jesus loved him; and within a few weeks of that time Peter got the blessing, and we find him winning three thousand souls in a single day.

Again, Satan may tell you that if you do get the blessing people will not believe that you have it. Well, suppose that they do not, what then? Will you refuse to believe God because people will not believe you? If you get the blessing, and live in the joy and sweetness and power and glory of it, they will have to believe you sooner or later, just as people have to believe there is a fire in the stove when they feel it.

To get the blessing you must resist the devil, and believe that it is for you.

4. You must believe that it is for you *now.* It is astonishing how sinners wish to put off the time of salvation, and it is even more astonishing how saved people put off seeking a clean heart until some other time. The devil and their evil hearts of unbelief keep saying, ' Some time, but not just now.' But the dear Lord in mercy keeps whispering, ' Behold, now is the accepted time; behold, now is the day of salvation '

(2 Cor. vi. 2). 'To-day if ye will hear His voice, harden not your hearts' (Heb. iii. 15). Nothing grieves the Holy Spirit and hardens the heart like this delay of unbelief.

5. The next thing to do is to come to Jesus for the blessing with a true heart, holding back nothing, but giving your all to Him for time and eternity that He may give His all to you. At this point there must be no hypocrisy, no double-dealing, no half-heartedness, no holding back part of the price. The Lord offers us the biggest blessing this side of Heaven. He offers us perfect cleansing from sin, perfect victory over the devil, and the Holy Spirit to dwell in our clean hearts to teach and guide and comfort us; but in exchange He asks us to give Him our little all.

How infinitely and hopelessly foolish shall we be if we are so selfish or fearful or unbelieving as to refuse! It is as though a king should offer a poor beggar garments of velvet and gold in exchange for rags, diamonds in exchange for dirt, and a glorious palace in place of a cellar or garret. How foolish would the beggar be who would insist on keeping a few of his rags, a little handful of his dirt, and the privilege of going back to his cellar now and again, until the king finally withdrew all the splendid things he had offered! And yet so foolish, and more so, are they who try to get this blessing from God while refusing to consecrate their all and obey Him fully.

The Lord's word to us on this point is: 'Bring ye all the tithes into the storehouse, that there may be meat in Mine house, and prove me now herewith, saith the Lord of Hosts, if I will not open you the windows of Heaven, and pour you out a blessing, that there shall not be room enough to receive it' (Mal. iii. 10). It is no little blessing, but an overflowing one that the Lord means to give you.

When Jonathan Edwards, one of God's mighty men of the past, was but a boy-student, he wrote as follows in his diary:

' I have this day solemnly renewed my covenant and dedication. I have been before God, and given myself and all that I am and have to Him, so that I am not in any respect my own, and can claim no right to myself —to this understanding, to this will, these affections; and have no right to this body—to this tongue, these hands, these feet; no right to these senses. I have given every power to God, so that for the future I will claim no right to myself.'

Does such a life seem unattractive to you? Some one has written:

'A cathedral window seen from without is dull and meaningless; but enter, and the light of Heaven streaming through it glorifies it with every beauty of form and colour. Consecration to God for service may seem dull enough when seen from without, but enter into that experience and the light of the divine love streaming through it will glorify your life with a beauty and blessedness which are Heaven's own.'

To make such a consecration we may have to go over it several times and assure ourselves that we have given all, and that we mean it with all our heart. But, having done this until we can look up into the face of Jesus without a doubt, and sing—

> My all is on the altar,
> I'm waiting for the fire—

we may be sure we are near the blessing.

If we thus give ourselves to God, there is but one thing more to do; that is, to take it by faith and wait patiently on Him for the witness of the Spirit that it is ours.

A nobleman whose son was sick came to Jesus ' and besought Him that He would come down, and heal his son: for he was at the point of death. Then said Jesus unto him, Except ye see signs and wonders, ye will not believe. The nobleman saith unto Him, Sir, come down ere my child die. Jesus saith unto him, Go thy way; thy son liveth. And the man believed the word

that Jesus had spoken unto him, and he went his way '
(John iv. 47-50). The next day when he got home he
found his boy well. Hallelujah! That is the kind of
faith that walks off with the blessing.

Jesus will not fail you at this point if you patiently
look to Him and hold fast your faith.

Again and again I have seen people burst into the
light when they have consecrated their all and believed
in this way. Some time ago in a holiness meeting the
Penitent-form was full of seekers among whom were
several earnest young men. I asked one of them who
seemed to be the most deeply in earnest: ' Do you now
give yourself and your all to God? '

' Yes, I do,' he said.

' Well, whose man are you, then ? ' I inquired.

' I am the Lord's.'

' Can you trust the Lord to sanctify His own man ? '

' Yes, I can.'

' When ? '

' Now! ' and he burst into the holy joy of faith and
began to praise the Lord at once; and several others
got the blessing that morning in the same way.

You too, my brother, my sister; you can have the
blessing just now if you thus meet the conditions.

> Faith, mighty faith, the promise sees,
>   And looks to that alone;
> Laughs at impossibilities,
>   And cries, ' It shall be done!

CHAPTER IV

WHEN CAN WE BE MADE HOLY?

A BRIGHT young soldier got up in one of my meetings several years ago and said, ' After the Lord converted me I did not want any bad thing, but there was something in me that did.'

A little boy of my acquaintance got blessedly saved and was very happy and good for some time. But one day he came to his mother and said, ' Mamma, I'm tired of living like this.'

' Why, what is the matter now? ' asked the mother.

' I want to be good all the time,' said the little fellow. ' You tell me to go and do things, and I go and do them; but I feel angry inside. I want to be good all the time.'

Both the young man and the boy were converted. Each wanted to be good, but each found in himself something wrong, and he knew that while that something remained, he was not holy. However correct the outward life might be, the heart was not clean. This is the experience of every converted person who has not pressed on into holiness, and it corresponds to the Scripture in which Paul says, ' When I would do good, evil is present with me ' (Rom. vii. 21).

When we are converted, our sins are forgiven and we feel a sweet peace within. We love God and man, and want to do good and be good all the time. We have power to do good, and to overcome bad habits and temptation, but there is still something in our hearts that needs to be removed before we are holy. That something within, the Bible calls ' the old man.' It is the old nature that gets angry when people or things do not suit us; that is deceitful, and proud, and unclean, and disobedient, and silly, and selfish. Of course, conversion gives a great blow to this ' old man '; subdues him, and makes him behave himself, so that he no longer acts so badly as he once did. But he is still alive, and watching his chance to get the victory again. And, sad to say, he often does get the victory, causing converted people to do and say things that are wrong and that grieve and quench the Holy Spirit. The ' old man ' causes quarrels and jealousies, envyings and evil speakings, in churches and in corps; and leads to backslidings of all kinds and the ruin of many Christian lives. Paul had a corps (see 1 Cor. iii.) that was greatly troubled in this way.

Before we can be holy, this ' old man ' must be ' put off,' this evil within must die, this seed of all sin must be destroyed, and this is something that can and does take place just as soon after conversion as we see the need and the possibility of its being done, and come to Jesus with all our heart, and with perfect faith to have it done.

Some people say that we cannot get rid of this evil nature until we die; but we must be guided by the Bible and believe that supremely. And the Bible certainly teaches that we can be made holy in this life. The Bible says, ' Be ye holy '; and that means now, not after death. If a man says to his boy, ' Be honest, be truthful,' he means: Be honest and truthful now, for *this* world, not in Heaven only. And so God means that we must be holy here and now.

Again the Bible says, ' Put off . . . the old man, which is corrupt . . . and put on the new man, which after God is created in righteousness and true holiness ' (Eph. iv. 22, 24). We are told to ' put off all these; anger, wrath, malice, blasphemy, filthy communication out of your mouth ' (Col. iii. 8). And we are told to ' be filled with the Spirit ' (Eph. v. 18). All this is to take place now.

We read of the disciples who ' were all filled with the Holy Ghost ' (Acts ii. 4), and of ' Stephen, a man full of faith and of the Holy Ghost ' (Acts vi. 5), and of believers whose hearts were purified by faith (Acts xv. 9) long before they got to Heaven. God is no respecter of persons; and just as He gave this great blessing to the early Christians, He will surely give it to us when we give ourselves fully to Him.

I shall never forget how one Sunday afternoon, after hearing of the possibility and blessedness of a pure heart, a beautiful girl of sixteen walked straight out to the Penitent-form, fell on her knees and, lifting her face to Heaven with tears, told the Lord how she wanted a clean heart filled with the Holy Spirit just then. She saw that she need not wait, but that *now* was the accepted time. And oh! how God blessed her. Soon the smiles were chasing away the tears and the joy of Heaven was shining on her face. Years after, I found her on the platform, a Lieutenant, with her face still shining and her heart still cleansed.

And so, my dear young comrade, this priceless blessing may be yours. Jesus has died to purchase this uttermost salvation, and it is your Heavenly Father's will for you just now. Have faith in God, give yourself utterly to Him, even now, and begin to seek the blessing with a determination never to stop seeking till it is yours, and you will not be long without it. Praise the Lord!

> Saviour, to Thee my soul looks up,
>   My present Saviour Thou!
> In all the confidence of hope,
>   I claim the blessing now.
>
> 'Tis done: Thou dost this moment save,
>   With full salvation bless:
> Redemption through Thy Blood I have,
>   And perfect love and peace.

CHAPTER V

HOLINESS: A LOVE SERVICE

'I WISH I knew the secret of Paul's piety,' said that good man, Asa Mahan, to Mr. Finney who replied : ' Paul said, " The love of Christ constraineth us ".' Just then the glorious truth burst upon his mind that we are sanctified not by works, but by faith which works by love; that the religion of Jesus is not one of vows and resolutions, terrible struggle and effort, but of life and power and joyous love; and he went out of Finney's room saying, ' I see it, I see it! ' From that hour his life was one of triumphant holiness.

Oh, that all men would see this—that the way of holiness is a ' new and living way,' not an old, dead, tiresome, heart-aching, heart-breaking way of forms and ceremonies that leave the soul still baffled and unsatisfied, and with a sense of failure and defeat! It is a way of victory and joy.

The simple secret of this ' new and living way ' is the constraining love of Christ. When we realize that He loves us, died for us, wants from us a service of love, and we then give ourselves up heartily, in faith, to such a love service, the secret becomes ours.

' Shall I have to go and tell mother and my brothers and the corps how inconsistent I have been ? ' asked a lassie with whom I was talking about the blessing. ' I don't feel that I can ever do that.' She had been defeated again and again by fits of temper, and I felt that she ought to confess to those whom she had probably hindered by her inconsistency. But I saw that she would not get the blessing by doing it because she *must*, but because she *wanted* to, out of very love for

Jesus, her mother, her brothers, and the corps. So I quietly replied that the Lord did not want a slavish service from her, but a love service; and that if she felt it would really do any good to make such a confession, and loved Jesus enough to do it to please Him, and to help those whom she had wronged by an inconsistent life, God would be pleased with it, but otherwise not. I assured her that if she did it in that spirit she would find it a joy.

After some further conversation we knelt to pray. She told the Lord all about herself, asked Him to cleanse her heart and fill it with His Spirit and love, and then she claimed the blessing. Here is a note I received from her several weeks later:

'I am very happy in the possession of a clean heart. Through God I have been able to gain victories that before I thought were absolutely impossible. The confessions that I told you I could not make, I only waited until the next day to make, and for the very love of it too, as you said I would. It has not been easy—anything but that; but such a burden has gone from my heart that I am happy even in the hardness. I fell one night through my old temper and felt as though my heart would break; but God forgave me, and showed me through that how weak I was; for I had almost thought that we could not fall after receiving the blessing. I suppose God took that way to show me that unless I trusted in Him I should fall. However, at the present time there is no shadow between the Lord and me, and I am happy.'

Have you, my dear comrade, been serving the Lord blindly and slavishly, simply because it is your duty, and yet with a constant feeling of unrest and unfitness? Oh, how He loves you, and wants to catch your ear, and win your heart, and draw you into a glad love service!

'But I am so weak and faulty, I have failed so often. Surely, the Lord must be discouraged with me,' you say. No, no, not if you are in earnest, any more than your mother was discouraged with you when, as a little toddler just learning to walk, you fell again and again. She did not cast you off, but picked you up, kissed the knees and nose that were bumped and loved you more than you dreamed. And in all your other failures she still bore with you and hoped for you. So it is with Jesus. Let this love constrain you. 'We love Him, because He first loved us' (1 John iv. 19). Trust Him. Give yourself wholly and heartily to Him, be sure you serve Him for love, and you will have learned the secret of a holy, happy life.

> Oh, let Thy love my heart constrain,
>   Thy love for every sinner free;
> That every fallen soul of man
>   May taste the grace that found out me;
> That all mankind with me may prove
> Thy sovereign, everlasting love!

CHAPTER VI

HOLINESS AND THE SANCTIFICATION OF THE BODY

THE prophet Isaiah says that God inhabits eternity (Isa. lvii. 15); and Solomon says, 'The heaven and heaven of heavens cannot contain Thee' (1 Kings viii. 27). But, wonder of wonders! Paul says that we are a habitation of God. 'What?' says he, 'know ye not that your body is the temple of the Holy Ghost which is in you?' (1 Cor. vi. 19). And again, 'Know ye not that ye are the temple of God, and that the Spirit of God dwelleth in you?' (1 Cor. iii. 16).

This is a very solemn truth, but it ought to be a joy-giving one. It certainly adds dignity and honour to us beyond anything that earthly rulers could possibly bestow, and it lifts our bodies from their kinship to the beasts into a sacred fellowship with the Lord. This fact makes the sanctification of the body both a glorious privilege and an important duty.

Many people think that sanctification, or holiness, has to do only with the soul. But the truth is, that it has to do with every part of our nature and every article of our possession. The body is to be sanctified as well as the soul. Paul wrote to the Thessalonians as follows: 'The very God of peace sanctify you wholly; and I pray God your whole spirit and soul and body be preserved blameless unto the coming of our Lord Jesus Christ' (1 Thess. v. 23). By this he means that the body is to be set apart and kept as a holy thing for the Lord.

We are to make a present of our bodies to the Lord.

Paul says, ' I beseech you therefore, brethren . . . that ye present your bodies a living sacrifice, holy, acceptable unto God ' (Rom. xii. 1). Just as the soldier surrenders his personal liberty, and gives his body to his country for hard campaigns, for toilsome marches, for weary sieges and, if need be, for death, so we are to present our bodies to the Lord. Jesus gave His body for us and we are to give our bodies to Him.

Not only are we to present our bodies as a whole to the Lord, but each member as well; the eyes, the ears, the hands, the feet, the tongue, each and all are to be given to Him. (See Rom. vi. 13.)

The eyes are to be turned away from the things that would wean the soul from God. This will include companionships and pursuits which, not evil in themselves, may become a hindrance to spiritual growth. The good is so often the enemy of the best.

Some years ago silver bracelets were very fashionable, and a girl who had plenty of money went to buy a pair. But before she found any pretty and dainty enough to suit her she got saved, and then she knew she had no right to spend her money foolishly, or to wear such things even if she had them. But her eyes had got into the habit of searching shop windows in every city where she went for those bracelets, and she found that the habit was very bad for her soul. It made her care less to pray, hindered her thinking about Jesus when she was out walking, and actually lessened her desire to get souls saved. So she had to give her eyes up to God to be kept from leading her away from Jesus; and for years afterward she said she never began a day without praying David's prayer, ' Turn away mine eyes from beholding vanity ' (Ps. cxix. 37).

It was a longing look toward the fertile plains of Sodom and Gomorrah that led to all the sorrows and losses of Lot. It was a covetous look at the Babylonish garment and wedge of gold that led to the utter ruin of Achan. It was a lustful look that led to the sad downfall and shame of David.

c

There are some things that a Christian should not look at, and if by chance his eyes should fall upon them, they should be turned away quickly lest sin should get into his heart through eye-gate. Every one who wishes to be holy will say with Job, ' I made a covenant with mine eyes ' (Job xxxi. 1).

Again, the ears are to be sanctified. The holy man will guard himself lest sin enter into his heart through ear-gate. ' Take heed what ye hear,' said Jesus (Mark iv. 24); and again, ' Take heed *how* ye hear ' (Luke viii. 18). Just so surely as the body can be poisoned or nourished and strengthened by the things we eat according to whether they be good or bad, so surely can the soul be poisoned or nourished by the things we hear. No pure-minded man or woman, boy or girl, will listen to an impure story, an obscene song, or unclean talk.

Some time ago, two Salvation Army officers were travelling by train. The railway carriage was crowded and they were separated. One of them sat down by an elderly man, and in a short time they were in conversation with a gentleman in front of them. Soon the elderly man looked about and said, ' There are no women near who can hear, are there ? I want to tell a story.' The officer was at once on guard, and said, ' I am a Salvationist, sir. I do not wish to hear a story that would be unfit for ladies to hear.' The old man looked ashamed, the gentleman in front looked a look of wonder, and the nasty story was not told. The Salvationist, no doubt, escaped a great temptation.

But while we should not listen to evil, neither should we speak it. Sometimes it is impossible to avoid hearing wicked and filthy things, however much we may wish to do so, for we cannot control the tongues of others. That was one of the sorrows of Lot in Sodom. His soul was ' vexed with the filthy conversation of the wicked ' (2 Pet. ii. 7). While we cannot control the tongues of others, we must control our own, and while we may not be able always to avoid hearing wicked and evil and unclean things, we can avoid saying them.

If we would be holy and enjoy God's smile, we must sanctify our tongues and keep our lips pure. ' Let no corrupt communication proceed out of your mouth, but that which is good to the use of edifying, that it may minister grace unto the hearers ' (Eph. iv. 29). We must not forget, however, that the heart is the fountain from which flows all our talk, and if that be clean the conversation will be pure. Jesus said, ' Out of the abundance of the heart the mouth speaketh ' (Matt. xii. 34). Therefore, ' keep thy heart with all diligence; for out of it are the issues of life ' (Prov. iv. 23).

> Take my voice, and let me sing
> Always, only for my King;
> Take my lips, and let them be
> Filled with messages from Thee.

Let the feet also be given to the Lord, no longer to walk in the ways of sin, but to walk patiently and gladly in the path of duty, and to run on errands of mercy.

> Take my feet, and let them be
> Swift and beautiful for Thee.

The hands are to be used for holy service, and no longer to smite and pilfer.

> Take my hands, and let them move
> At the impulse of Thy love.

Thus the whole body is to be given to the Lord and kept and used for Him. Since Jesus ascended to Heaven, He has no body upon earth. So, will you prove your love to Him, my comrade, by letting Him have yours ? If so, no sexual impurity is to be allowed, no unclean habit is to be indulged, no appetite is to be permitted to gain the mastery; but the whole body is to be kept under and made the servant of the soul.

Athletes, football and cricket players, and prize-fighters when in training, are exceedingly careful about their health. They select their food with care and eat nothing that would disagree with them, omitting heavy suppers; they abstain from strong drink and tobacco;

c*

they bathe their bodies daily; they go to bed and get up at regular hours; they sleep with open windows and, of course, have plenty of fresh air and systematic exercise. This they do for months, sometimes for years, simply that they may beat some other fellows in contests of strength and skill. ' Now they do it,' says Paul, ' to obtain a corruptible crown; but we an incorruptible.' And then he adds, ' I keep under my body, and bring it into subjection: lest that by any means, when I have preached to others, I myself should be a castaway ' (1 Cor. ix. 25, 27).

I know a man who noticed that when he ate too much he became irritable and was subject to various temptations from which a careful diet freed him. He had to control his appetite in order to keep a clean heart.

Young people are likely to squander their health in all sorts of useless and careless ways, and are tempted to laugh or sneer at their elders when they lift a warning voice. But they will some day find that advance in holiness, progress toward Heaven and happiness and usefulness, are more dependent on the right care of the body than they supposed.

' Beloved, I wish above all things that thou mayest prosper and be in health, even as thy soul prospereth ' (3 John 2).

> Let my hands perform His bidding,
>   Let my feet run in His ways,
> Let mine eyes see Jesus only,
>   Let my lips speak forth His praise.
>   All for Jesus,
>   Let my lips speak forth His praise.

CHAPTER VII

HOLINESS AND UNCONSCIOUS INFLUENCE

SOME people often sing:

Oh, to be nothing, nothing;

but, in reality, to be *something*, to be useful, is one of the first and strongest desires that spring up in the heart of a truly saved person. And one of the blessed things about a holy life is its supernatural, constant, and unconscious influence for good. A holy person does not have to resolve and struggle to be a blessing. Without conscious effort, his life and talk and looks inspire the faint-hearted, encourage the timid, instruct the ignorant, feed the hungry, and rebuke the proud, selfish and wayward. He blesses people in all sorts of ways without at the time knowing it, and is often surprised to learn how the Lord has been using him.

Of Jesus, Luke says that ' the whole multitude sought to touch Him: for there went virtue out of Him, and healed them all.' (Luke vi. 19). And, just so, virtue goes out from holy people as perfume floats out from a rose, or warmth from fire, or light from a flame.

A sanctified officer said to a comrade who was deserting his post, ' I feel that woe is me if I preach not the Gospel.' Some weeks later an officer said to him, ' I overheard you that day when you said, " Woe is me if I preach not the Gospel," and it stirred my soul and made me feel that way too.' Those words had been said quietly, but God was in them, and they were with power. This fits Solomon's saying, ' The words of wise men are heard in quiet more than the cry of him that ruleth among fools ' (Eccles. ix. 17).

A number of years ago in America, two sanctified Salvationists, a man and his wife, were followed home from their meetings several nights by a nurse from the hospital nearby. She could not get away from her duties long enough to attend the meetings, but she said to herself, ' I will walk home behind them, and maybe I shall get something for my soul.'

And she did. All unconscious that a hungry heart was feeding upon their words, the Salvationists talked out of their clean hearts about Jesus; His love, His word, His uttermost salvation; and as a result the nurse was so filled with desire to glorify God and save souls that she left her work for people's bodies, became a missionary, and is now in the far East. This strange story came back, from Korea, to the two Salvationists after many days, to surprise and gladden them, and fill them with wonder at the unconscious power of holy conversation.

The very silence of a holy man is with power. I have known such silence to still the voice of slander and foolishness, and hush the laugh of silliness and folly. An officer with a clean heart aflame with love met a girl who had offered herself for our Goodwill work. She was giggling and chattering in a way that convinced him that instead of being filled with the Holy Spirit she was empty. He wanted to speak to her about her soul, but hardly knew how to begin, so he was silent, and prayed in his heart for her. Afterward she said, ' I looked at his face and said to myself, " There is a holy man, a man dead to sin. But I am alive yet." ' And that sight of his face led her to seek and find the blessing, and now, for years she has been a most useful and devoted officer. The very presence of such a man is a rebuke to sin and half-heartedness and folly, and is a mighty inspiration to goodness.

After the overthrow of Sisera and all his host, Deborah and Barak sang a song of triumph and thanksgiving, and closed it with these words, ' Let them that love Him be as the sun when he goeth forth in his

might' (Judges v. 31). Think of it! How mighty the
sun is! how it floods the world with light! how it melts
the snow and thaws the iceberg, warms the whole earth
and quickens and gladdens every living thing! None
can stop it in its course; and so God means that it shall
be with holy men and women. They comfort those
that are right and convict those that are wrong, just as
the sun energizes everything that has life and hastens
the dissolution of everything that is dead.

But while holy people have power to bless and do
good, they also have a strange influence often to arouse
persecution. They prove the sayings of Jesus, ' I came
not to send peace, but a sword' (Matt. x. 34).

But even this will turn to a blessing. God makes it
work for good to them that love Him, and it often leads
to the salvation of the persecutors. The godly life and
testimony of Joseph rebuked his unclean brothers, and
they sold him into slavery. But years after, when he
ruled over all Egypt, and his brothers were seeking his
forgiveness and mercy, he said, ' Fear not: . . . as for
you, ye thought evil against me; but God meant it unto
good, to bring to pass, as it is this day, to save much
people alive' (Gen. l. 19, 20). Thus persecution often
leads to the salvation of many people.

This very power of a holy life to arouse hatred and
persecution and opposition is a part of the unconscious
influence of holiness, and is mightily used by God for
the advancement of His kingdom on earth, so that
many have been able to say with Paul when he was put
into jail, that locking them up had only made the
Gospel spread more, and made other men bolder to
preach it.

' Come,' said a distinguished Scots professor to a
German sceptic, ' and I will show you a student who
will make you think of Jesus.'

' There is no difference between him and the Book,'
said his fellow-townsmen of a Chinese convert.

' Ye are the light of the world,' said Jesus; ' ye are
the salt of the earth.'

Such lives are full of healing, cleansing, helping, comforting power; and such may be your life, my brother, my sister, no matter how dark your surroundings, if you will consecrate yourself entirely to God, take up your cross and follow Jesus, and seek, ask for, and receive the Holy Spirit as your Sanctifier.

Oh, that He may come into your heart just now, and nevermore be grieved, or allowed to depart!

> Oh, make my life one blazing fire
> Of pure and fervent heart desire
> The lost to find, the low to raise,
> And give them cause Thy name to praise,
> Because wherever I may go
> I show Thy power to every foe!

CHAPTER VIII

HOLINESS AND HUMILITY

THOSE who oppose holiness often say that we who profess it are proud, and that the doctrine tends to spiritual pride. But the truth is, that holiness goes down to the root of all pride and digs it up utterly. A holy man is one who has found himself out, and pronounced judgment against himself, and come to Jesus to be made every whit whole. And so long as he keeps the blessing he is deeply humble.

God said to Israel by the Prophet Ezekiel, 'Then shall ye remember your own evil ways, and your doings that were not good, and shall loathe yourselves in your own sight for your iniquities and for your abominations' (Ezek. xxxvi. 31).

This is a certain effect of entire sanctification. The sinful heart apologizes for itself, excuses inbred sin, favours it, argues for it. A man who still has the carnal mind says, ' I think one ought to have a little pride. I would not give a snap of my finger for a man who had not some temper. A man who will not stand up for his rights is weak.' And so he excuses and argues in favour of the sin in his own heart.

Not so the man who is holy. He remembers his former pride and loathes himself for it, and longs and prays to sink deeper and deeper into the infinite ocean of his Saviour's humility until every trace and stain of pride are for ever washed away. He remembers his hasty temper and hates it. He cries day and night for the perfect meekness of the Lamb of God who, like a sheep dumb before her shearers, opened not His mouth, while His enemies worked their fiendish will; and, so far from smiting back, would not even talk back, but prayed, ' Father, forgive them.'

He sees the beauty of God's holiness and loves it. He sees the full extent of his former corruption and acknowledges and loathes it. Before, he thought man had some natural goodness, but now he knows and confesses that ' the whole head is sick, and the whole heart faint. From the sole of the foot even unto the head there is no soundness in it; but wounds, and bruises, and putrifying sores' (Isa. i. 5, 6).

He sees his own evil ways. At one time he thought that there was not one holy man on earth, for he could see a mote in every man's eye; but now he discovers that there are many holy men, and the mote which he was sure he saw in his neighbour's eye he now finds to have been the shadow of the beam that was in his own eye.

An earnest, sanctified man once said to me, ' There are certain sins I once thought it was morally impossible for me to commit, but the Holy Spirit has shown me the awful deceitfulness of my heart, and I now see that before He cleansed me there were in me the seeds of all iniquity, and there is no sin I might not have committed, and no depth of moral degradation to which I might not have sunk, but for the restraining grace of God.'

One who has thus seen the plague of his own heart may be cleansed in the precious Blood and have a holy heart, but he will never say to another, ' Stand by thyself, come not near to me; for I am holier than thou' (Isa. lxv. 5); but, remembering his own former condition, he will point him to the Lamb of God which taketh away the sins of the world.

True humility makes a person particularly attractive to God. Listen to what Isaiah says, ' Thus saith the high and lofty One that inhabiteth eternity, whose name is Holy; I dwell in the high and holy place, with him also that is of a contrite and humble spirit, to revive the spirit of the humble, and to revive the heart of the contrite ones' (Isa. lvii. 15).

Jesus said, ' Whosoever shall exalt himself shall be abased; and he that shall humble himself shall be exalted ' (Matt. xxiii. 12); and James said, ' God resisteth the proud, but giveth grace unto the humble ' (Jas. iv. 6).

' Do you wish to be great? ' asks Augustine, ' then begin by being little.'

' Whosoever therefore shall humble himself as this little child,' said Jesus, ' the same is greatest ' (not shall be, but ' *is* greatest ') ' in the Kingdom of Heaven ' (Matt. xviii. 4).

Here are some of the marks of a truly humble person.

1. A truly humble soul does not take offence easily, but is ' pure, then peaceable, gentle, and easy to be intreated, full of mercy and good fruits, without partiality, and without hypocrisy ' (Jas. iii. 17).

2. He is not jealous of his position and dignity, or quick to resent what seems to touch them. Before the disciples were sanctified they found a man who was casting out devils in the name of Jesus, and they took offence because he did not follow them; and forbade him. Self is very sensitive. ' But Jesus said, Forbid him not' (Mark ix. 39).

One day the Spirit of the Lord rested on two men in the camp of Israel in the wilderness, and they prophesied. 'And there ran a young man, and told Moses. . . . And Joshua . . . the servant of Moses, said, My lord Moses, forbid them. And Moses ' (the meekest of men) ' said unto him, Enviest thou for my sake? Would God that all the Lord's people were prophets, and that the Lord would put His Spirit upon them! ' (Num. xi. 27–29).

3. A truly humble person does not seek great things for himself, but agrees with Solomon when he says, ' Better it is to be of an humble spirit with the lowly, than to divide the spoil with the proud ' (Prov. xvi. 19). He rejoices in lowly service, and is more anxious to be faithful to duty and loyal to principle than to be renowned among men.

The disciples were often disputing among themselves which should be the greatest, but Jesus washed their feet as an object lesson, and commanded them to become servants of one another if they would be great.

4. Humble people are modest in dress. They think more of ' the ornament of a meek and quiet spirit ' (1 Pet. iii. 4) than of the clothes they wear. They will endeavour always to be clean and neat, but never fine and showy.

5. They are also plain and simple in speech. They seek to speak the truth with clearness and accuracy and in the power of the Holy Spirit, but never with ' great swelling words ' and bombast, or with forced tears and pathos that will arouse admiration for themselves. They never try to show off. To them it is painful to have people say, ' You are clever,' ' That was a fine speech.' But they are full of humble, thankful joy when they learn that through their words some sinful soul was saved, some erring one corrected, or some tempted one delivered. They speak not to please men, but their heavenly Master; not to be applauded, but to feed hungry hearts; not to be admired of men, but to be approved of God.

And, on the other hand, their humility keeps them from criticizing and judging those who have not these marks of humility. They pray for such people, and leave all judgment to God who, in His own time, will try every man's work by fire (1 Cor. iii. 13).

' Be clothed with humility: for God resisteth the proud, and giveth grace to the humble ' (1 Pet. v. 5).

> Anger and sloth, desire and pride,
> This moment be subdued;
> Be cast into the crimson tide
> Of my Redeemer's Blood.

CHAPTER IX

HOW TO KEEP HOLINESS

DO you ask, ' How can I keep the blessing? '

1. Do not let your poor heart be burdened with the thought that you have to do it all yourself. In this, as in all else, you are only a worker together with God. He loves you more than a mother loves her little child, and He is going to help you to keep the blessing. Remember that the blessing is simply the result of His indwelling in your heart, and you are not to think so much about keeping the blessing as about keeping Him.

It will not be a hard matter to keep Him in your heart if you are in earnest, for He wanted to get there when you were a sinner, and He certainly desires to stay there as long as you will let Him; and if you will let Him, He will keep you.

One of our leading officers, who is a personal friend of mine, once told me that when he first heard the doctrine of holiness he felt that he could not be holy while engaged in worldly business. But one day he read the prayer of Jesus, ' I pray not that Thou shouldest take them out of the world, but that Thou shouldest keep them from the evil ' (John xvii. 15). He saw at that moment that God *could* keep him, and he sought and found the blessing, and has been rejoicing ever since.

Oh, how it rested me and comforted my heart one day when, sore tempted by the devil, I read these words, ' Now unto Him that is able to keep you from falling, and to present you faultless before the presence of His glory with exceeding joy ' (Jude 24). I saw that He was able to keep me, and I knew that He was willing. My heart rested on the promise and, bless Him, He does keep me.

' Fear thou not; for I am with thee: be not dismayed; for I am thy God: I will strengthen thee; yea, I will help thee; yea, I will uphold thee with the right hand of my righteousness' (Isa. xli. 10).

Paul got fairly jubilant over the keeping power of God—it was his boast when he wrote, ' Who shall separate us from the love of Christ? Shall tribulation, or distress, or persecution, or famine, or nakedness, or peril, or sword? . . . Nay, in all these things we are more than conquerors through Him that loved us. For I am persuaded, that neither death, nor life, nor angels' (fallen angels, or devils), ' nor principalities, nor powers' (no combination of devils or men), ' nor things present, nor things to come, nor height' (of prosperity), ' nor depth' (of adversity), ' nor any other creature, shall be able to separate us from the love of God, which is in Christ Jesus our Lord' (Rom. viii. 35, 37–39).

Paul trusted God to keep him and so must we. We should surely fall if God withheld His help for a moment.

But James tells us that ' faith without works is dead '; and so we must not only trust God, but must work together with God if we would keep the blessing.

2. To keep the blessing you must keep all upon the altar. What you have given to the Lord you must not take back. You gave all to get the blessing and you must continue to give all to keep it.

> My all is on the altar,
> I'll take it back no more,

must be your motto and your song. The devil will try to get you to come down from the cross; the world will allure you, the flesh will cry out against you, your friends may weep over you, or frown upon you, or tease and torment, or threaten you; some of your comrades will criticize you and doubt you, but you must stick to Jesus, and take nothing back that you have given to Him. There is usefulness, and peace, and God's smile, and a crown, and a kingdom before you, but only condemnation, and ruin, and Hell behind.

A little heathen boy in Africa heard a sermon about Jesus and His tender dying love and saving power, and he gave himself fully to the Lord and Jesus came into his heart. This so enraged his heathen father that he said, ' I'll get this Jesus out of him; I'll beat Him out.' And he beat the little fellow most cruelly.

But the boy was still true. Then the father said, ' I'll smoke this Jesus out of him.' So he put the boy into a hut, shut up the opening in the roof and nearly smothered him with smoke. That failed also, and then he tried starvation; he gave the boy nothing to eat for several days. All persecution failed, however, and the little fellow remained true. He had given all to Jesus, and he would take nothing back. When asked how he had endured all the terrible trials he had passed through, he quietly said, ' I just stuck to Jesus.'

3. If you would keep the blessing, you must be quick to obey God. I do not mean by this that you are to get into such haste that you will not take time to think and pray about all that you do. God wants you to use your head and your heart and all the good sense He has given you. He wants you to take time to speak to Him, to consider and find out His will; but once you have found it out, if you would have His smile and favour, and keep the blessing, you must not delay, but obey at once. Oh, the losses of peace and power, joy and sweet communion with God that people suffer through hesitation at this point! Like Felix, they wait for ' a convenient season ' which never comes! and, like Felix, they lose all. ' Strike while the iron is hot.' ' Make hay while the sun shines.' ' Put out to sea while the tide is in.' Do as Abraham did. God told him to sacrifice Isaac as a burnt-offering—Isaac, the joy of his house, the light of his eyes, the hope of his old age, the treasure of his heart! He did not parley and delay, but ' rose up early in the morning . . . took

Isaac his son . . . and went unto the place of which God had told him ' (Gen. xxii. 3).

A salvation soldier who was greatly used of God told me that he was one day reading a half-religious novel. He had reached a most thrilling point in the story when the Holy Spirit seemed to say to him, ' Stop reading this at once and you will never regret it.' He said that he closed the book at once, put it down and never opened it again, and such a blessing came into his soul as he was hardly able to contain. Years after, when he told me this, he was still rejoicing that he had promptly obeyed the voice of the Lord and left that sort of thing for ever.

If you have lost the blessing through a failure promptly to obey, do not be utterly discouraged, but begin over again and the Lord will restore you. But do not trifle with God again; pray and believe for His help to obey lest a worse thing come upon you.

4. If you would keep the blessing you must not depend upon your feelings, but as a friend of mine used to say, ' Stand by your facts.' Young Christians are very likely to be betrayed into mistakes by their feelings —by their happy feelings as well as their unhappy ones.

When they are happy they are in danger of thinking themselves better than they are, of not watching and praying as they should; and when they are not happy they are likely to get discouraged, cast away their confidence in the Lord, and conclude that it is useless for them to try to be holy. The safest way is to pay attention to your facts and let your feelings take care of themselves.

If people are kind to you, and your digestion is good, and your sleep sound, you will probably feel well. But if people are unkind, and the east wind blows, and you eat something that lies heavy in your stomach, and your sleep is broken by horrid dreams, you will probably not feel well; but in neither case is your relation to God changed. Your facts are just the same. If you have given yourself to God, and have taken nothing back, but can look up into His dear face and say, ' My all is on the altar, and I trust in Thee,' then you are His, and your business is to stand by that fact, and trust that the Blood keeps you clean.

When you are happy, sing songs, and when you are heavy-hearted pray, and try and sing a little too, and never cast away your confidence, for there is a great reward before you, if you hold fast.

5. One of the greatest helps to keeping the blessing is for two or three young people who have it to meet together as often as possible to read the Bible, and pray with and encourage each other. This can usually be done just before or between the meetings on Sunday. This practice helped me more than anything else, I think, when I first got the blessing. Put a burning coal or stick by itself and the fire will often go out, and it will be cold and black; but put several sticks or coals together and they will burn brightly. And so it is with hearts full of holy fire.

At such little meetings it is well to unite in prayer for others whom you are eager to see converted or to enter into the blessing and, as you see them getting saved and sanctified, this will add mightily to your own faith and love.

Finally, whole-hearted and continued consecration and self-denial, earnest prayer, joyful and diligent study of God's word, deep humility before the Lord, aggressive work for others, and humble definite testimony to the blessing, will surely establish us in holiness, and keep us from falling.

> How blest are they who still abide
> Close sheltered in Thy bleeding side !
> Who life and strength do thence derive,
> And for Thee fight, and in Thee live.

CHAPTER X

HOLINESS AND ZEAL FOR SOULS

'FOLLOW Me, and I will make you fishers of men,' said Jesus to Peter and Andrew; and now, as then, when Jesus saves a soul, that soul wants to catch men, wants to see others saved. Holiness increases this desire and makes it burn with a quenchless flame.

The zeal of other people blazes up, burns low, and often dies out, but the zeal of a man with a clean heart, full of the Holy Ghost, increases year by year. Others run away from the prayer meeting, but he holds on. Others do not grieve if souls are not saved, but he feels that he must see souls saved or die. Others are zealous for 'big goes,' tea parties, ice-cream suppers and musical festivals, but nothing pleases him so much as a prayer meeting where souls are crying to God for pardon and cleansing, and others are shouting for joy.

And this zeal for the salvation and sanctification of men leads him to do something to reach them. He lets his light shine. He speaks to people not only from the platform and the pulpit at long range, but he button-holes them and speaks to them wherever he finds them. Holiness makes it easy for him to do this. He loves to do it. He finds that, as he follows the Spirit, the Lord fills his mouth with truth and gives him something to say.

A number of years ago a young man full of the Holy Ghost stopped a few minutes at a watering trough to give his horse a drink, and at the same time a stranger rode up to water his horse. For about five minutes that young man with a heart overflowing with love told the stranger about Jesus. Then they separated to meet no more in this world; but the stranger was converted to God as a result of that five minutes of faithful, personal dealing, and became a soul-winner in Africa. He often wondered who that Heaven-sent young man was who pointed him to Jesus. One day in Africa he received a box of books from America, and on opening a small volume of memoirs there he saw the face and the name of the man to whom he owed his soul's salvation and whose cry to God was, ' Give me souls, give me souls, O Lord, or I cannot live.'

There are two things for us to remember:

1. Most sinners hope that some one will speak to them about their soul.

' Why did you not speak to me about my soul? ' asked a student of his room-mate.

' I thought you would not like it,' was the reply.

' Why, that was the reason I roomed with you,' said he.

A father prayed earnestly in the meeting for the salvation of sinners. After the meeting, he and his boy walked home a mile away. The boy hoped his father would speak to him about Jesus and salvation, for he was under deep conviction, but not a word did the father say. Then the boy said within himself, 'After all, there is nothing in religion,' and he became a reckless unbeliever; all because his father did not speak to him about his soul.

Poor sinners! They often laugh and make merry when their hearts are wellnigh breaking with sorrow or conviction, and they are only waiting for some one to point them to Jesus to be saved.

2. When God moves us to speak to people, we may be sure that He has been dealing with their hearts and preparing the way for us. When the Lord sent Philip to speak to the Ethiopian, He had the Ethiopian all ready for Philip's message.

A friend of mine in Cleveland used to meet a certain railroad conductor almost every day. The conductor was a big, splendid fellow, but a sinner. One day my friend felt he ought to speak to that conductor about his soul. He was a small man and trembled and ran away like Jonah, and for the next three weeks he was disobedient and in great misery. Every day he would meet the conductor, and the Lord would say, ' Speak to him about his soul.' After three weeks of agony he went out of his office one day, and lo! there was that conductor again. He could stand it no longer. He braced himself, buttoned up his coat and said, ' Lord, help me! I will speak to him if he knocks me down.' Then he spoke, and to his surprise and shame and joy, the big man burst into tears, and said, ' I have really been wanting some one to speak to me about my soul for three weeks.'

God is faithful; He had been to that man before He sent my friend to him. And there are hungry souls all around us like that one.

Again, holiness not only makes us eager for the salvation of sinners, but fills us with unutterable longings for the perfecting of the saints. We want to see every man perfect in Christ Jesus. I have never known any one get the blessing without this desire following.

Oh, how God longs to have a holy people on earth! Will you give yourself to Him, my brother, my sister, to help Him get such a people ? You can be a yoke-fellow with Jesus, a worker with God. Will you ? If so, begin just now to pray for the one you feel God would have you help to save or sanctify, and you will be working with Jesus, and, if you continue, great shall be your reward.

> Not my own! My time, my talents,
>   Freely all to Christ I bring,
> To be used in joyful service
>   For the glory of my King.

CHAPTER XI

HOLINESS AND WORRY

WORRY is a great foe to holiness, and perfect trust puts an end to worry. ' I would as soon swear as fret,' said John Wesley. The murmuring and complaining of His children have ever been a great sin in the sight of God, and led to untold suffering on their part.

Most people do not see this to be a sin, but it is. It dishonours God, blinds the eyes to His will, and deafens the ears to His voice. It is the ditch on one side of the pathway of trust. Lazy or heartless indifference is the ditch on the other side. Happy is the Christian who keeps out of either ditch and walks securely on the pathway. Though it be often narrow and difficult, it is safe. Praise the Lord!

Worrying prevents quiet thought and earnest believing prayer, and it is, therefore, always bad. If circumstances are against us we need quietness of mind, clearness of thought, decision of will, and strength of purpose with which to face these circumstances and overcome them. But all this is prevented or hindered by fret or worry.

First, we should not worry over things that we can help, but set to work manfully to put them right. Sir Isaac Newton, one of the greatest of men, laboured for eight years preparing the manuscript of one of his great works, when one day he came into his study and found that his little dog, Diamond, had knocked over a candle and burned all his papers. Without a sign of anger or impatience, the great, good man quietly remarked,

'Ah, Diamond, little do you know the labour and trouble to which you have put your master!' and without worrying sat down to do that vast work over again.

Second, we should not worry over the things we cannot help, but quietly and confidently look to the Lord for such help as He sees best to give. There is no possible evil that may befall us from which God cannot deliver us, if He sees that that is best for us; or give us grace to bear, if that is best. Holiness of heart enables us to see this. An accident befell a little child I heard of, and for twenty-four hours endangered its life. The sanctified mother did all she could, then committed her darling to the Lord and peacefully awaited the issue. Within twenty-four hours the danger was passed; the child was safe. An old coloured auntie who had witnessed the calm trust of the mother said, ' You certain is de queeres' woman I ever see! Here dis chile been in danger ob its life for twenty-four hours and you not worried a bit!'

' Well, auntie,' said the mother, ' I couldn't trust the Lord and worry too; so I did what I could and trusted, and you see that all is well. And I have had the peace of God in my heart for twenty-four hours.'

Paul says, ' Be careful for nothing; but in everything by prayer and supplication with thanksgiving let your requests be made known unto God. And the peace of God, which passeth all understanding, shall keep your hearts and minds through Christ Jesus ' (Phil. iv. 6, 7). Again, Isaiah says: ' Thou wilt keep him in perfect peace, whose mind is stayed on Thee: because he trusteth in Thee ' (Isa. xxvi. 3).

Our business is, then, always to pray, give thanks for such blessings as we have, keep our minds stayed on God, and worry about nothing.

Holiness makes a man so sure of the presence and love and care of God that, while doing with his might what his hands find to do, he refuses to worry and sings from his heart:

I will trust Thee, I will trust Thee,
All my life Thou shalt control;

and he is certain that while he trusts and obeys, neither
devils nor men can do him real harm, nor defeat God's
purpose for him.

The heart realization of Heavenly help, of God's
presence in time of trouble, of angels encamping round
about them that fear Him, is the secret of a life of
perfect peace in which anxious care is not shunned, but
joyously and constantly rolled on the Lord who ' careth
for us '; who bids us cast our care on Him. Are you
poor, and tempted to worry about your daily bread?
God sent the ravens to feed Elijah, and later made him
dependent upon a poor widow woman with only
enough flour and oil to make one meal for herself and
her child. But through long months of famine God
suffered not that flour to waste, nor that oil to fail.

The God of Elijah is the God of those who trust in
Him for evermore. Now such trust is not a state of lazy
indifference, but of the highest activity of heart and
will; it is both a privilege and a duty. Of course, only
such a perfect trust can save from undue anxiety, but
this trust is an unfailing fruit of the Holy Spirit dwelling
in a clean heart. And we can only keep this trust by
always obeying the Holy Spirit, strict attention to daily
duty, watchfulness against temptation, and much
believing, persevering, unhurried prayer.

Has some one talked unkindly or falsely about you?
Don't worry, but pray, and go on loving them and
doing your duty, and some day God will ' bring forth
thy righteousness as the light, and thy judgment as the
noon-day ' (Ps. xxxvii. 6).

Are you sick? Don't worry, but pray. The Lord
can raise you up (Jas. v. 15); or make the sickness work
for good (Rom. viii. 28) as He did for a sister I knew in
Chicago. For five years she was helpless in bed with
rheumatism, but her five big sons were converted
during that time, and she was so happy that she would
not have had those five years spent in any other way.

Have your own wrongdoings brought you into trouble? Don't worry, but repent to the very bottom of your heart, trust in Jesus, walk in your present light, the Blood will cleanse you, and God will surely help you.

Are you troubled about the future? Don't worry. Walk with God to-day in obedient trust, and to-morrow He will be with you. He will never fail you nor forsake you.

> If our trust were but more simple,
>   We would take Him at His word,
> And our lives would be all sunshine
>   In the sweetness of our Lord.

CHAPTER XII

HOLINESS AND DUTY

IF holiness delivers us from worry it increases the sense of duty and of personal responsibility. It was the holiness of His heart that led the twelve-year-old boy Jesus to say to His mother, ' Wist ye not that I must be about My Father's business? ' (Luke ii. 49). To Him the world was not a playground only, but a field of labour. His Father had given Him work to do and He must do it before the night came in which no man can work.

By this I do not understand that He was continually engaged in ceaseless, grinding toil with no hours of recreation and rest. We know that in after years He went away with His disciples to rest awhile. He took time to enjoy the flowers, to consider the lilies, to watch the sparrows, to view the grass of the field. But He neglected no duty. He did not slight nor shirk His work. He was no trifler. He was honest. What He did He did well, and with His might. And this spirit always accompanies true holiness of heart.

Most people divide the work of the world into what they call sacred and secular work. Preaching, praying, reading the Bible, conducting meetings and the like, they consider to be sacred work; but washing and ironing and learning, building houses and making shoes, practising law or medicine, working in mines and mills, in shops and stores, and on shipboard; that they call secular work.

But why make such a distinction ? It is not the work, but the heart and purpose behind the work at which God looks. The Salvation Army officer, or minister,

or missionary who works for the salary he gets, or for
the social position he enjoys, or for an opportunity for
study and travel and personal culture, has a secular
heart and makes his work secular; while the farmer or
lawyer, washerwoman or cook, shoemaker or miner, or
stenographer who has a holy heart, and who does good
work as unto the Lord, makes his or her work sacred.

The time was when a man built his own house, made
his own shoes, sheared his sheep and gave the wool to
his wife who dyed it, spun, and wove it, and made it
into clothes for her household. He raised corn and
meat and prepared it for food, and so they lived inde-
pendent of the world on the fruits of their own toil.
But times have changed. Society is now a great
organism in which there are a thousand different occu-
pations, and people must needs divide the work between
them. And now God wants each to be faithful and holy
and happy where he is, doing his own work faithfully as
Jesus would do it.

A poor German woman in Massachusetts used to
say, ' I'm a scrubbing-woman and a missionary by the
grace of God.' She went to the homes of the rich to
scrub and clean, and she testified of Jesus everywhere
she went. She scrubbed to pay expenses, and preached
the Gospel, and she scrubbed well that the Gospel
might not be despised or blamed.

They tried to arrest Paul in Damascus after his conversion, but he was let down through a window by the
wall in a basket and so escaped. Some one has said
that possibly one of the early Christians made the rope
that held the basket; that by making a good rope he
saved Paul's life. So, in his humble way, without
knowing it, he helped in all the mighty missionary
labours and salvation warfare of Paul. But what if he
had carelessly made a poor rope that had broken with
Paul!

We know not what part of our work God is going to
use in His plans for saving the world; therefore, let it all
be good and true.

We are God's tools. He is the Workman. I took an axe to cut down a tree; but I took a tiny gimlet to bore a hole in a piece of furniture I wished to mend. I could not cut down the tree with the gimlet, nor bore the hole with the axe, and yet both pieces of work were important. So the Lord has different kinds of work for which He must have different kinds of workmen.

The General stirs the world and lifts it toward God. You, perhaps, teach a few ragged boys. Do not despise your work or be discouraged. You are as important to God as the gimlet was to me. Do your duty. Do it as though Jesus were in the class you teach, by the bench where you work, in your kitchen, office, store, or mill. Do it without murmuring. Do it gladly and He may take it up, and make it a part of His great plan long after you have laid it down as he did the rope which saved Paul. Never mind what your work is. Moses tended sheep. Jesus was a carpenter. Paul was a tent-maker. Gideon was a farmer's man. Dorcas was a dressmaker; Martha was a housekeeper; Luke a doctor; Joseph and Daniel were governors and statesmen; in every relation of life and in all duty they were faithful, or we should not have heard of them.

If you are true, you will ' adorn the doctrine of God ' our Saviour in all things, you will have the sweet approval of your own conscience, the smile of God, and however humble your work may have been, if you are steadfast unto the end, you will some day hear Him say, ' Well done, good and faithful servant; thou hast been faithful over a few things, I will make thee ruler over many things; enter thou into the joy of thy Lord ' (Matt. xxv. 23). Hallelujah!

True promotion which is from God, both in this world and that which is to come, is the reward of faithfulness over little things and few, as well as over great and many, and if you have the experience of holiness you will be faithful.

You must not, however, be anxious about the reward. That is largely deferred into the next world. It is your duty and mine to be faithful, to be faithful unto death. If reward is delayed, it will be all the greater when it comes, be assured of that. God will see to it that your treasure which you lay up with Him bears compound interest. What a surprise to the man that made that rope if he finds at the Judgment Day that he had a share in the wealth piled up by Paul's labours!

There is one part of the reward, however, that is never delayed, that is, happiness and contentment and God's favour.

In service which Thy love appoints
  There are no bonds for me;
My secret heart is taught the truth
  That makes Thy children free;
A life of self-renouncing love
  Is one of liberty.

CHAPTER XIII

HOLINESS AND PRAYER

Thou art coming to a King,
Large petitions with thee bring,
For His grace and power are such
None can never ask too much.

PRAYER is a puzzle to unbelievers but a sweet privilege to us. A stranger will hesitate to approach a king, but the king's child will climb on to the king's knee, and whisper in the king's ear, and ask all sorts of favours of the king; and get them, too, because he is his child. Now that is the secret of prayer.

When we have repented of sin, given ourselves to God and been born again, we are His dear children, and we have a right to come to Him in prayer. The devil will try to hinder us and, if our faith is weak, we may doubt and hesitate; but God invites. He wants us to come, to come with all our wishes, cares, burdens, sorrows, perplexities, everything. Nothing that is of interest to us is too small to interest Him. Many people do not believe this, but it is true. They think God is interested only in big things; but the same God that made the flaming suns and mighty worlds made the tiny insect, fashioned the lenses of its little eye and painted with brightest colours its dainty wing. He is interested in the little quite as much as in the great, therefore we may bring everything to Him in prayer.

I once heard a very intelligent old saint, past fourscore years of age, say that though she moved into a flat by herself she was never alone. Jesus kept company with her and they were able to talk together over the simplest of everyday occurrences. She was right, and people who think God does not want His children to be so familiar as that are wrong, and have much yet to learn.

We should be definite, and pray for what we want. A Christian told me the other day that she could come to God for a clean heart, but not for a new dress. She was wrong. If she seeks ' first the Kingdom of God, and His righteousness,' she has just as much right to lay before the Lord her need of a new dress as of a spiritual blessing. Of course, spiritual blessings are by far the most important and should be sought first; but Jesus wants us to talk to Him about everything, and bring to Him all our wants. Let this sink deep into your heart if you would be holy, and happy, and useful.

For many days there had been no rain in Ohio, the fields were parched and brown, and everything cried out for water. The people were anxious and knew not what to do. One Sunday, before his sermon, Mr. Finney prayed for rain. One who heard that prayer reported it after twenty-three years, and said it was as fresh in his mind as though he had heard it but yesterday. Finney told the Lord all about their great need, and among other things said, ' We do not presume to dictate to Thee what is best for us, yet Thou dost invite us to come to Thee as children to a father, and tell Thee what we want. *We want rain.* Our pastures are dry. The cattle are lowing and wandering about in search of water. Even the little squirrels in the woods are suffering for the want of it. Unless Thou dost give us rain our cattle must die, for we shall have no hay for them for winter, and our harvests will come to naught. *O Lord, send us rain, and send it now!* Although to us there is no sign of it, it is an easy thing for Thee to do. *Send it now*, Lord, for Christ's sake! ' And the Lord sent it. Before the service was half over the rain came in such torrents that the preacher's voice could not be heard; so with tears of wonder and joy and thanksgiving, they sang:

When all Thy mercies, O my God,
My rising soul surveys,
Transported with the view I'm lost
In wonder, love, and praise.

Finney took God at His word and dared to ask for what he wanted. He used to say, ' Lord, I hope you do not see that I can be denied.'

Many people pray for things they want, but James tells us that they do not get them because they ask amiss, to consume them upon their lusts. They want things for worldly pleasure or profit, or for sinful, selfish purposes (Jas. iv. 3).

The secret of prevailing prayer is this; that we are so in love with Jesus, so at one with Him, that we do not want anything to use or spend in any way that would grieve Him. I want a new suit of clothes. What for? That I may strut around in pride, or to show myself off to the people I know? No, no, but that I may be suitably clothed for my work for God. I want food. What for? To strengthen me for sinful, selfish pleasures and labours? No, no, but to glorify God. I want a clean heart. What for? That I may be happy and get to Heaven? No, no, not that alone, but that I may honour God and help Him win others to love and trust and obey Him. When I want things in that spirit, then the Lord can trust me with anything for which I ask Him, for I will not ask Him for anything that is not for His glory. If I am in doubt about anything being for His glory, then I will ask Him to give it to me only if He sees it is best to do so.

Again, we must pray in faith. It is sad, it is heart-breaking, the way people doubt God, the cold, lifeless prayers they utter before Him! You would not want a friend to come to you for anything you had promised to give, with such faithless asking, would you? God is much more willing to give good things to us than we are to give good gifts to our children. And we should come with lively faith that will not be denied. The promise is, ' What things soever ye desire, when ye

pray, believe that ye receive them, and ye shall have
them ' (Mark xi. 24). Bless the Lord!

Do you ask, ' How can I get faith? ' I answer,
through God's Word. Look up His promises, and go
to God with them, and say with David, ' Remember
the word unto Thy servant, upon which Thou hast
caused me to hope ' (Ps. cxix. 49). That is what
Finney did. He wanted rain, and he went to God with
the promise, ' When the poor and needy seek water,
and there is none, and their tongue faileth for thirst, I
the Lord will hear them, I the God of Israel will not
forsake them ' (Isa. xli. 17).

But again, we must persevere in prayer. We must
hold on to God and not let go till the answer comes, or
until God shows us why it does not come. Sometimes
the answer to prayer comes at once. The first person I
remember praying with after God sanctified me got the
blessing at once.

One morning I prayed for a suit of clothes which I
very much needed. A great peace came into my heart
and I got off my knees laughing, knowing that God had
heard and answered my little request. How and when
the suit was to come I did not know. After breakfast I
went out, and when I returned a man was waiting for
me to go to the tailor's and be measured for the best
suit in his shop. I knew absolutely nothing about this
when I prayed, but God did.

But sometimes the answer is delayed. At such times
we must not fold our hands and idly conclude that it is
not God's will, but instead, search in our hearts to make
sure the hindrance is not in us, and still continue to
plead with God, and in due time the answer will come.

Hold on to God for the salvation and sanctification of
your loved ones and God will hear and answer you.
Wrestle with Him, give Him no rest, remind Him every
day of His promise and your burning desire, and He
must hear and answer you.

A young man prayed for a friend for thirteen months
and finally died without seeing him saved. But God

was faithful and remembered the prayers of His child.
In due time that friend was converted and became a
martyr for Christ in Africa.

Finally, we should mingle thanks with our prayers,
even before we see the answer. ' In everything by
prayer and supplication with thanksgiving let your
requests be made known unto God,' wrote Paul (Phil.
iv. 6). A mother got gloriously sanctified at an Army
Penitent-form, and then began to pray in faith for the
conversion of her daughter. For some time she prayed,
but one day she said, ' Lord, I am not going to pray for
this any longer, but I am going to thank Thee for the
salvation of my child.' Within a week the girl was
saved, and is now an officer.

Holy people are in vital union and partnership with
God, and their prayers, inspired by the Holy Spirit,
move all Heaven in their behalf. Then the only reason
why they accomplish so little is because they ask so
little, and with such feeble faith. ' Men ought always
to pray, and not to faint,' said Jesus (Luke xviii. 1).
Will you, my comrade, give yourself up to a life of glad,
persevering, believing prayer? If so, you will be one
of God's princes on earth.

> Behold the Throne of Grace,
>   The promise calls me near.
> There Jesus shows a smiling face,
>   And waits to answer prayer.
>
> My soul, ask what thou wilt,
>   Thou canst not be too bold;
> Since His own Blood for thee He spilt,
>   What else can He withhold?